Creative Mind and Success

CREATIVE MIND
AND SUCCESS

Updated And Gender-Neutral

❖   ❖   ❖

Ernest Holmes

newt
LIST

Chicago • New York

Contents

Part 2
Practice
113

Part 1

Instruction

❖   ❖   ❖

AN INQUIRY INTO TRUTH

❖   ❖   ❖

An inquiry into truth is an inquiry into the cause of things as the human race sees and experiences them. The starting point of our thought must always being with our experiences. We all know that life *is*, otherwise we could not even think that we are. Since we can think, say, and feel, we must be. We live, and we are conscious of life, so we and life must be. If we are life and self-knowing consciousness, then it follows that we must have come from life and consciousness. We start, then, with this simple fact: Life is, and life is conscious.

What is the nature of this life? Is it physical, mental, material, or spiritual? A little careful thinking based on logic, rather than any merely personal opinion, does much in clearing up some of these questions that at first seem to stagger us with their bigness.

How much of that which exists may we call life? The answer would have to be that life is all that there is. It is the reason for all that we see, hear, and feel—for all that we experience in any way. Nothing from nothing leaves nothing, and it is impossible for something to proceed from nothing. Since something exists, that from which it came must be all that is. Life, then, is all that there is. Everything comes from it, including us.

The next question is, "How do things come from life?" How do the things that we see come from the things that we do not see? The things that we see must be real, because we see them. To say they are not real will never explain them or answer any question about them. God's work is not a world of illusion, but one of divine realities. The truth must not explain away things that we see. It must explain what they are. We are living and experiencing varying degrees of consciousness and conditions. Only when the *why* of our life and of our experience is understood will we know the least thing about the truth.

Jesus did not say that things are illusions. He said that we must not judge from the standpoint of the seen, but must judge righteously, or with right judgment. He meant that we must get behind the appearance and find out what caused it. We must not in any way fool ourselves or allow ourselves to believe we have been fooled. We are living in a world of realities. Whatever we have experienced is a reality as far as that experience is concerned, although if we had had a higher understanding of life, the unpleasant experience might have been avoided.

WHAT LIFE IS

❖   ❖   ❖

What do we mean by life? Life is that which we see, feel, hear, touch, or taste, and the reasons for them. We must come into contact with all we know of life. We have already realized what life is, otherwise we could not have had any of these experiences.

"In the beginning was God," or life. Out of this life, everything that exists is made. Therefore, life must flow through all things. There is no such thing as dead matter. Life is a unity, and it cannot be changed except into itself. All forms are forms of this unity and must come and go through some inner activity. This inner activity of life, or nature, must be some form of self-consciousness, or self-knowing. In our human understanding, we would call this inner knowing, or consciousness, *thought*. The Spirit—life, or God—must make things out of itself through self-recognition, self-knowing, or, as we would call it, *thinking.*

Since God is all, there is nothing to hinder God from doing what God wishes. So the question "How do things come into being?" is answered by saying, "God makes things out of itself." God thinks, or knows, and the thing that it thinks or knows appears from itself and is made out of itself. There is no other possible explanation for what we see. Unless we are willing to begin here, we will never understand how it is that things are not material, but spiritual.

HUMANKIND'S PLACE IN CREATION

❖   ❖   ❖

Where does humankind come in? Humankind *is*. Therefore, it follows that we, too, are made out of God since God, or Spirit, is everything. Being made out of God, we must partake of God's nature because we are "made in God's image."

Humankind is the center of God in God. Whatever God is in the universal, humankind must be in the individual world. The difference between God and humankind is one of degree, not of quality. We are not self-made. We are made out of God.

Why did God do this? No living person can answer this question. It is something that is known only by the Creator. We might suppose that humankind was made to live with and be enjoyed by God, to be one with the Spirit. It is true that those who have felt this most deeply have had a corresponding spiritual power that leads us to suppose that God really did make humankind as a companion. Humankind is the individual, and God is the universal. "As the Creator has life within itself." Our mind is made out of God's mind, and all that we are or ever will be, all that we have or ever will have, must partake of the divine nature. Humankind did not make it so, but it is so, and we must accept that fact and see what we can do with it.

If we have the same power in our individual lives that God has in the universal, then this discovery will mean freedom from all bondage when we learn how to use this power. As God governs the universal world, so we will govern our individual world, always subject to the greater law and life. This could not be otherwise if we realize what follows from it, because so realizing, we find ourselves living in a very different world from the one in which we thought we were living. God governs not through physical law as result, but first by inner knowing. The physical then follows. In the same way, humankind governs its world by the process that we call the power of our thought.

Our inner life is one with the Creator. There can be no separation because there is logically nothing to separate us from God. There is nothing but life. The separation of two things implies putting a different element between them. Since there is nothing different from God, the unity of God and humankind is firmly established forever. "My Creator and I are one" is a simple statement of a great soul who perceived life as it really is and not from the mere standpoint of outer conditions.

Taking as the starting point that we have the same life as God, it follows that we use the same creative process. Everything is one, comes from the same source, and returns again to it. "The things that are seen are not made of the things that do appear." What we see comes from what we do not see. This is the explanation of the entire visible universe and is the only possible explanation.

As God's thought makes worlds and peoples them with all living things, our thought makes our world and peoples it with all the experiences we have. By the activity of our thought, things come into our life. We are limited, though, because we have not known the truth. We have thought that outside things control us, but the truth is that we have always had the thing inside us that could have changed everything and given us freedom from bondage.

The question naturally arises, "Why did God create us and make us free agents?" If God had created us in such a way as to compel us to do or to be anything that was not of our choosing, we would not be individuals at all; we would be machines. Since we know that we are individuals, we know that God made us this way, and we are just discovering the reason. When we wake up to this fact—the greatest truth of all time—we will find that it answers all questions. We will be satisfied that things are what they are. We will perceive that we may use our God-given power to work, to think, and to live so that we will in no way hinder the greater from operating through us. According to the clearness of our perception and greatness of our realization of this power, we will provide within ourselves. There will no longer be a sense of separation, but in its place will come that divine assurance that we are one with God. This is how we will find our freedom from all suffering, whether it is that of the body, mind, or world.

The Beginning of Understanding

❖   ❖   ❖

We are beginning to realize that we have life within ourselves as the great gift of God to us. If we really have life, if it is of the same nature as the life of God, if we are individuals and have the right of self-choice that constitutes individuality, then it follows that we can do with our life what we want to do. We can make out of ourselves that which we wish. Freedom is ours, but this freedom is with law and never outside it.

We must obey law. If we disobey it, it still must act as law and, so acting, has to punish us. This we cannot change, but must submit to. Freedom comes to each one of us from understanding the laws of our own lives and conforming to them, thereby subjecting them to our use, with the goal of health, happiness, and success.

Law obtains throughout all nature, governing all things, both the seen and the unseen. Law is not physical or material, but mental and spiritual. Law is God's method of operation. We should think of God as the great Spirit whose sole impulse is love, freely giving of itself to all who ask and refusing none. God is our creator in every sense of the term, watching over, caring for, and loving all the same. While all is love, in order that things may not be chaotic, all is also governed by law. As far as you and I are concerned, this law is always mental.

OUR CONDITIONS
GOVERNED BY OUR THINKING

❖　❖　❖

It is easy for the average person to see that mind can control and, to a certain extent, govern the functions of the body. Some go even further and see that the body is governed entirely by consciousness. We can see this without much difficulty, but it is not so easy for us to see how thought governs our conditions and decides whether they are to be successes or failures.

If our conditions are not controlled by thought, by what then are they controlled? Some say that conditions are controlled by circumstances. But what are circumstances? Are they cause, or are they effect? Of course, they are always effect. Everything that we see is an effect. An effect is something that follows cause, and we are dealing with causation only. Effects do not make themselves, but are held in place by mind, not by causation.

If this does not answer the question, begin over again and realize that behind everything that is seen is the silent cause. In your life, you are that cause. There is nothing but mind, and nothing moves except as mind moves it. We agree that while God is love, your life is governed absolutely by mind, or law. In our lives of conditions, we are the cause, and nothing moves unless our mind moves it.

The activity of our mind is thought. We are always acting because we are always thinking. At all times, we are either drawing things to us or pushing them away from us. In the ordinary individual, this process goes on unconsciously, but ignorance of the law will excuse no one from its effects.

Someone might ask, "Do you think that I wanted to fail?" Of course not! But according to the law, which we cannot deny, you must have thought that failure might come or in some way you let the thought into your mind.

Thinking back over the reason for things, we will find that we are surrounded by a mind, or law, that casts back to us, manifested, everything we think. If this were not true, we would not be individuals. Individuality means only the ability to think what we want to think. If that thought is to have power in our lives, then there has to be something that will manifest it. Some are limited and bound by law through ignorance. This law, sometimes called *karma*, is the law that binds the ignorant and gives freedom to the wise.

We live in mind, and it can return to us only what we think into it. No matter what we may do, law will always obtain. If we think of ourselves as poor and needy, then mind has no choice but to return what we have thought into it. At first, this may be difficult to realize, but the truth will reveal that law could act in no other way. That which we think is the pattern, and mind is the builder. Jesus, realizing this law, said, "It is done unto you even as you have believed." *It is done unto you.* There is nothing to worry about, because it is done unto you. With a tremendous grasp of true spiritual thought, Jesus manifested bread and wine from the ethers of life. He never failed to teach that when we know the truth, we are freed by that knowledge.

Unconscious Creation

❖ ❖ ❖

I once had a patient who was suffering from a large growth. This patient was operated on and had about fifty pounds of water removed. In a few days, the growth had returned. Where did it come from? Not from eating or drinking. It did not move from one part of the body to another part, because that would not have increased the patient's weight. It must have been created from elements that the patient took in from the air. It had to come from something not physically seen, something appearing from nothing that we can see. What we call "creation" is the same thing—the visible appearing from the invisible. Was this patient's growth a creation?

Cases as remarkable as this occur every day. We

should not deny this fact, but try to explain it. In the case of this patient, there must have been an activity of thought molded into form; otherwise, how could this growth have appeared? There is nothing manifest unless there is a cause for the manifestation. Investigation proves that behind every condition, whether of body or environment, there has been some thought, conscious or unconscious, that produced the condition. In the case of this patient, the thought was not conscious. Creation is going on all the time. We should realize this and learn how to control it so that we will create the things that we desire and not those that we do not want. The Bible says, "With all your getting, get understanding."

Jesus understood all this, and it took no more effort for him to do what he did than it is for us to breathe or to digest our food. Jesus understood. That is all. Because Jesus understood and used these great laws with objective consciousness, people thought he must be God. When something unusual occurs today, people think that a miracle has been performed. Jesus was not God. He was a manifestation of God, and so are all people. "I say you are gods, and every one of you children of the Most High."

In view of all this, a thinking person will be compelled to admit that creation is first spiritual through mental law, and then physical in manifestation.

We do not really create. We use creative power that

already exists. Relatively speaking, we are the creative power in our own lives, and as far as our thought goes, there is something that goes with it that has the power to bring forth into manifestation the thing thought of. Before now, we have used this creative power in ignorance and have brought on ourselves all kinds of conditions. But today, many people are beginning to use these great laws of their being in a conscious, constructive way. This, then, is the great secret of all spiritual philosophy movements under whatever various names, cults, and orders. All use the same law, even though some deny real revelation. We should get into an attitude of mind in which we recognize the truth wherever we find it. The trouble with most of us is that unless we see sugar in a sugar bowl, we think it must be something else, so we stick to our petty prejudices instead of looking for principles.

First Steps

✦ ✦ ✦

The first thing to realize is that since thought manifests, it necessarily follows that all thought does the same.
If it didn't, then how would we know that the particu-
lar thought we are thinking is the one that will create?
Mind must either cast back all or none. Just as the creative
power of the soil receives all seeds put into it and immediately begins to work on them, so mind must receive all
thought and at once begin to operate upon it. So we find
that all thought has some power in our lives and over our
conditions.

We are making our environment by the creative power of our thought. God has created us this way, and we
cannot escape it. By conforming our lives and thoughts to

a greater understanding of law, we bring into our experience just what we wish, letting go of all that we do not want to experience and taking in the things we desire.

Every person is surrounded by a thought atmosphere. This mental atmosphere is the direct result of thought, which in its turn becomes the direct reason for the cause of that which comes into our lives. Through this power, we are either attracting or repelling. Like attracts like, and we attract to us just what we are in mind. It is also true that we become attracted to something that is greater than our previous experience by first embodying the atmosphere of our desire.

Every business, every place, every person, every thing has a certain mental atmosphere of its own. This atmosphere decides what is to be drawn to it. For instance, successful people do not go around with an atmosphere of failure. Successful people think about success. Successful people are filled with that subtle something that permeates everything they do with an atmosphere of confidence and strength. In the presence of such people, we feel as if nothing is too great to undertake. We are uplifted and inspired to do great things, to accomplish. We feel strong, steady, and sure. We feel a great power in the presence of such big souls.

Why do some people have this kind of effect over us, while others seem to depress, to drag us down, and in their presence we feel as though life is a load to carry? Because one type is positive and the other negative. In every physical respect these types are alike, yet one has a mental and spiritual power that the other does not have, and without that power, the individual can do very little.

Which of these two people do we like better? With whom do we want to associate? Certainly not those who depress us! We have enough of them already. The ones who inspire us with our own worth are those we turn to every time. Before we even reach them, in our haste to be near, even to hear their voices, we feel a strength coming to meet us. Do you think those people who have such wonderful powers of attraction will ever want for friends? Will they ever need to beg for a job? So many positions are already open to them that they are weighing in their minds which ones to take. They do not have to become successes. They already are.

Thoughts of failure, limitation, or poverty are negative and must be eliminated from our lives for all time. Some may say, "But what of the poor? What are you going to do with them? Are they to be left without help?" The same power is in them that exists in all people. They will be poor until they wake up and realize what life is. All the charity on Earth has not ended poverty, and it never will. If it could have, it would have done so long ago. It could not; therefore, it has not. It will do the poor a thousand times more good to show them how to succeed than tell them that they need charity. God has given us a power, and we must use it. We can do more toward saving the world by proving this law than all that charity has ever given it.

In the manifold world today, there is more money and provision than the world can use. Not even a fraction of the wealth of the world is used. Inventors and discoverers are adding to this wealth every day. But in the midst of plenty, surrounded by all the gifts of heaven, humankind sits and begs for daily bread. We must realize that we have brought these conditions on ourselves. Instead of blaming God, our neighbor, or the devil for the circumstances that surround us, we should seek the truth. We should tell everyone who will believe what their real nature is, show them how to overcome all limitations, give them courage, and show them the way. If they will not believe, if they will not walk in the way, it is not our fault. We have done all we can and must go our way. We may sympathize with people, but never with trouble, limitation, or misery. If people insist on clinging to their troubles, all the charity in the world will not help them.

Remember that God is the silent power behind all things, always ready to spring into expression when we provide the proper channel, which is receptive and positive faith in the evidence of things not seen with the physical eye, yet eternal in the heavens.

All is mind, and we must provide a receptive avenue as it passes out through us into the outer expression of our affairs. If we allow the world's opinion to control our thinking, then that will be our demonstration. If, on the other hand, we rise above the world, we will do a new thing.

All people are making demonstrations, but most of them are only making the ones they can make with their present powers of perception.

How to Attain Strength

✦   ✦   ✦

We must use the right attitude of mind in all that we do, filling ourselves with such courage and power of strength that all thought of weakness flees before us. If any thoughts of weakness should come, ask this question: Is life weak? If life is not weak and if God is not discouraged, then you are not, never were, and never will be. Sickly, discouraged thought cannot withstand this attitude of mind.

Life is strong, and you are strong with the strength of the Infinite. Forget everything else as you revel in this strength. You are strong and can say, "I am." You have been laboring under an illusion; now, you are not disillusioned. Now you know, and knowing is using the law in a constructive way. "I and the Spirit are one." This is strength for the weak and life for all who believe.

We can fill ourselves with the drawing power of attraction so much that it will become irresistible. Nothing can hinder things from coming to those who know that they are dealing with the same power that creates all from itself, moves all within itself, and yet holds all things in their places. Repeat this many times each day until you rise to that height: "I am one with the infinite mind."

In order to be sure that we are creating the right kind of mental atmosphere and attracting what we want, we must at first watch our thinking, unless we create that which we should not like to see manifest. In other words, we must think only what we wish to experience. All is mind, and mind casts back to us only what we think. Nothing ever happens by chance. Law governs all life, and all people come under that law. But we ourselves set that law in motion, and we do this through the power of our thought.

We each live in a world of our own making, and we should speak only such words and think only such thoughts as we wish to see manifested in our lives. We must not hear, think, speak, read, or listen to limitations of any kind. There is no way under heaven that we can think two kinds of thought and get only one result. It is impossible, and the sooner we realize it, the sooner we will arrive. This does not mean that we must be afraid to think, in case we create the wrong image, but it does mean that the way most people think can produce nothing but failure. That is why so few succeed.

Those who succeed will never let their minds dwell on past mistakes. They will forgive the past in their lives and in the lives of other people. If they make a mistake, they will forgive it at once. They will know that as long as they desire any good, there is nothing in the universe that opposes them. God does not damn anyone or any thing; people do.

God does not make things by comparing God's power with some other power. God knows that the word is spoken, and it is done. If we partake of the divine nature, we must know the same thing in our lives that God knows.

What We Will Attract

❖   ❖   ❖

We will always attract to us, in our lives and conditions, according to our thought. Things are only outer manifestations of inner mental concepts. Thought is
not only power, but it is also the form of all things. The
conditions that we attract will correspond exactly to our
mental pictures. It is quite necessary, then, that successful business people should keep their minds on thoughts
of happiness, which should produce cheerfulness instead
of depression. They should radiate joy and be filled with
faith, hope, and expectancy. These cheerful, hopeful at-
titudes of mind are indispensable to the one who really
wants to do things in life.

Put every negative thought out of your mind once

and for all. Declare your freedom. Know that no matter what others may say, think, or do, you are a success now, and nothing can hinder you from accomplishing your good.

All the power of the universe is with you. Feel it, know it, and then act as though it were true. This mental attitude alone will draw people and situations to you.

Begin to blot out, one by one, all false beliefs, all ideas that you are limited, poor, or miserable. Use that wonderful power of will that God has given you. Refuse to think failure or to doubt your own power.

See only what you wish to experience, and look at nothing else. No matter how many times the old thought returns, destroy it by knowing that it has no power over you. Look it squarely in the face and tell it to go. It does not belong to you, and you must know and stick to the truth that you are now free.

Rise up in all the faith of those who know what they are dealing with, and declare that you are one with infinite mind. Know you cannot get away from this mind and that wherever you may go, there, right beside you, waiting to be used, is all the power there is in the universe. When you realize this, you will know that in union with this power, you are more than anything that can ever happen to you.

More about the
Power of Attraction

❖   ❖   ❖

Always remember that Spirit makes things out of itself. It manifests in the visible world by becoming the thing that it wills itself to become. In the world of the individual, the same process takes place. We were given the use creative power, but with its use comes the necessity of using it as it is made to be used. If God makes things out of God's thought before they come into manifestation, then we must use the same method.

You can attract only that which you first mentally become and feel yourself to be in reality, without any doubting. A steady stream of consciousness going out into creative mind will attract a steady manifestation of conditions. A fluctuating stream of consciousness will attract the corresponding manifestation or condition in your life. We must be consistent in our attitude of mind, never wavering. The apostle James says, "Ask in faith, nothing doubting, for those who doubt are like a surge of the sea driven by the wind and tossed. For let not them think that they shall receive anything of the Lord."

We are all immersed in an aura of our thinking. This aura is the direct result of all that we have ever said, thought, or done. It decides what is to take place in our life. It attracts what is like itself and repels what is unlike itself. We are drawn toward those things that we mentally embody. Most of the inner processes of thought have been unconscious, but when we understand the law, all that we have to do is consciously embody what we wish and think of that only, and we will be silently drawn toward it.

We have this law in our hands to do with as we will. We can draw what we want only as we let go of the old order and take up the new, and this we must do to the exclusion of all else. This is an undertaking for the strong, self-reliant soul, and the end is worth the effort. Those who can hold their thoughts in focus are the ones who will obtain the best results.

This should not imply the necessity of strain or anything of a strenuous nature. On the contrary, strain is just what we must avoid. When we know that there is only one power, we will not struggle. We will know, and in calmness, we will see only what we know must be the truth. This means having a persistent, firm determination to think what we want to think, regardless of all outer evidence to the contrary. We look not to the seen, but the unseen. The ruler of Israel understood this when, looking on the advancing host of the enemy, he said, "We have no might against this great company, but our eyes are upon God"—upon the one power.

How to Attract Friends

❖   ❖   ❖

Those who have learned to love all people no matter who they may be will find plenty of people who will return that love to them. This not mere sentiment and is more than a religious attitude of mind. It is a scientific fact and one to which we should pay attention. The reason is this: Since all is mind and we attract to us what we first become, until we learn to love, we are not sending out love vibrations, and until we send out love vibrations, we cannot receive love in return.

One of our first tasks is to learn to love everyone. If you have not done this yet, begin to do it now. There is always more good in people than bad, and seeing the good tends to bring it forth. Love is the greatest healing and drawing power on Earth. It is the reason for our be-ing, which explains the importance of having something or somebody to love.

The life without love has not been lived. It is dead. Love is the sole impulse for creation, and those who do not have this great incentive have never developed the real creative instinct. No one can swing into the universal without love, because the whole universe is based on it.

If you find yourself without friends, you must send your thought out to the whole world at once, full of love and affection. Know that this thought will meet the desires of some other person who wants the same thing, and in some way, the two of you will be drawn together. Get over thinking that people are perplexing. That kind of thought will only produce misunderstand-ing and cause you to lose the friends you already have. Think of the whole world as your friend, but also be the friend of the whole world. In this way and with this sim-ple practice, you will draw to you so many friends that there will not be enough time to enjoy them all. Refuse to see the negative side of anyone. Refuse to let yourself misunderstand or be misunderstood. Do not be morbid. Know that everyone wants you to have the best. Affirm this wherever you go, and you will find things just as you wish them to be.

The atmosphere created by lovers of humankind is

so powerful that, although their short-comings may be many, the world will still love them. "To those who love much, much will be forgiven." People are aching for real human interest, for someone to tell them that they are all right. Which people do we like better? The ones who are always full of trouble and faultfinding, or the ones who look at the world as their friend and love it? We want the company of the person who loves and, in loving, forgets all else.

The only reason we think that other people are strange is because they do not happen to think as we do. We must get over this small, petty attitude and see the big picture.

Those who see what they want to see, regardless of what appears, will someday experience in the outer what they have so faithfully seen within.

For purely selfish motives alone, we cannot afford to find fault, hate, or even to hold in mind anything against any living soul. The God who is love cannot hear the prayer of the person who is not love. Love and cooperation are the greatest business principles on Earth. *God is love.*

We make our unity with all people, with all life. We affirm that God in us is unified with God in all. This one is now drawing into our life all love and companionship. We are one with all people, with all things, with all life. As we listen in the silence, the voice of all humanity speaks to us and answers the love that we hold out to it.

This great love that we now feel for the world is the love of God, and it is felt by all and returned from all. Nothing comes in between, because there is nothing but love. We understand all people, and that understanding is reflected back to us from all people. We help; therefore, we are helped. We uplift, and we are uplifted. Nothing can mar this perfect picture of ourselves and our relations with the world. It is truth. We are now surrounded by all love, all friendship, all companionship, all health, all happiness, all success. We are one with life. We wait in silence while the great Spirit bears this message to the whole world.

THE CONTROL OF THOUGHT

❖   ❖   ❖

Those people who can control their thoughts can have and do whatever they wish to have and do. Everything is theirs for the asking. They must remember that whatever they get is theirs to use but not to hold. Creation is always flowing by, and we have as much of it as we can take and use. Any more would cause stagnation.

We are relieved of the thought of clinging to anybody or anything. The great principle of life creates for us faster than we can spend and use. The universe is inexhaustible, it is limitless, and it knows no bounds and has no confines. We are not depending on a reed shaken by the wind to give us all that we want, have, or ever shall have, but on the principle of life itself. We are not affirming merely some power or a great power. It is *all* power. All that we have to do is believe this and act as though it were so, never wavering even once, no matter what happens. As we do this, we will find that things are steadily coming our way and that they are coming without the awful effort that destroys the peace for the majority of the race. We know that there can be no failure in the divine mind, and this mind is the power on which we are depending.

Just because we are depending on divine mind, we must not think that we do not have to do our share. God will work through us if we allow it, but we must act as if we are sure of ourselves. Our part is to believe and then act in faith.

Jesus went to the tomb of Lazarus believing and knowing that God was working through him. Often, when we have to go somewhere or do something, we know with deep conviction that there will be a power going with us that none can oppose. When we feel this secure place in our thought, all that we have to do is to act. There is no doubt that the creative power of the universe will answer, because it always does. We do not need to take the worry onto ourselves, but rather we "make known our requests with thanksgiving."

When Jesus said, "All things whatsoever you pray and ask for, believe that you receive them and you shall have them," he was uttering one of those many truths that were clear to him and that we are just beginning to see. He knew that everything is made out of mind, and that without the positive acceptance on the part of the individual, there is no mold into which mind can pour itself forth into form. In the mind of God, there is the correct mold, the true knowing, but in the mind of humankind, there is not always true knowing. Since God can do for us only by doing through us, nothing can be done for us unless we are positively receptive. When we realize the law and how it works, we will provide that complete inner acceptance. By doing so, we permit the Spirit to do the work, to make the gift.

The reason we can make our requests known with thanksgiving is because we know from the beginning that we are to receive, and so we cannot help being thankful. This grateful attitude to the Spirit puts us in close touch with power and adds much to the reality of the thing we are dealing with. Without it, we can only do a little. So let us cultivate all the gratitude that we can. In gratitude, we will send our thoughts out into the world, and as they come back, they will come laden with the fruits of the Spirit.

CREATING ATMOSPHERE

❖   ❖   ❖

To those who have realized that all is mind and that everything is governed by law, there comes the thought that we can create, or have created for us, from our own thinking. We can create such a strong mental atmosphere of success that its power of attraction will be irresistible. We can send our thought throughout the world and have it bring back to us whatever we want. We can fill our place of business with the power of success so completely that it will draw customers from far and near. Thought will always bring back to us what we send out. First, we must clear our thought of all unbelief.

Without mental clearness on the part of the thinker, no real creative work can be done. As water will reach its own level, so mind will return to us only what we first believe. We are always getting what we believe, but not always what we want. Our thought has the power in the outer form of conditions to reach an exact correspondence to our inner conditions.

By thinking, we set in motion a power that creates. It will be exactly as we think. We throw an idea into mind, and mind creates it and sets it on the path of our life. Think of it, then, as your greatest friend. It is always with you, wherever you may be. It never deserts you. You are never alone. There is no doubt, no fear, no wondering. You *know*. You are going to use the only power that there is in the universe. You are going to use it for a definite purpose. You have already fixed this purpose in your thought. Now, you are going to speak it forth.

You are speaking it for your own good. You desire only the good, and you know that only the good can come to you. You have made your unity with life, and now life is going to help you in your affairs.

You are going to establish in your mental rooms such an atmosphere of success that it will become an irresistible power. It will sweep everything before it as it realizes the greatness and all-mightiness of the One. You are so sure that you do not even look to see if it is going to happen; you *know*.

The word, which is one with the infinite life, is to

be spoken in calm, perfect trust. It is to be taken up, and at once it is to be operated on. Perfect is the pattern and perfect will be the result. You see yourself surrounded by the thing that you desire. Your word is now establishing it by perfect life, by infinite activity, by all power and by all guidance. The power of the Spirit is drawing to you all people. It is supplying you with all good. It is filling you will all life, truth, and love.

Wait in perfect silence while the inner power takes it up. Then, know that it is done unto you. There goes forth from this word the power of the infinite. "The words which I speak, they are Spirit, and they are life."

THE POWER OF WORDS

❖   ❖   ❖

Our word spoken forth into creative mind is endowed with the power of expression. "By our words, we are justified, and by our words, we are condemned." Our word has the exact amount of power that we put into it. This does not mean power through effort or strain, but power through absolute conviction or faith. It is like a little messenger who knows what to do and just how to do it. We speak into our words the intelligence that we are, and because our words are backed by that greater intelligence of the universal mind, our word becomes law for the thing that is spoken. Jesus understood this far better than we do. He absolutely believed it, because he said, "Heaven and earth shall pass away, but my words shall not pass away till they be fulfilled."

Our word is inseparable from absolute intelligence and power. If any word has power, it must follow that all words have power. Some words, according to our conviction, may have a greater power than others, but all words have some power. We should be very careful, then, about the words we speak.

We are one with the infinite mind, and our words have the power of life within them. The word is always with us, never far off. The word is in our own mouth. Every time we speak, we are using power.

We are one in mind with the whole universe. Each one of us is eternally united in this mind with real power. It is our own fault if, after knowing this, we do not use this truth.

We should feel ourselves surrounded by this mind, this great pulsating life, this all-knowing reality. When we feel this near presence, this great power and life, then all we have to do is to speak forth into it with all the positive conviction of the soul that has found its source. It will be done to us as we have believed.

A wonderful power of expression is waiting for those who truly believe. When we wake up to the real facts of being, we can attain anything. As yet, we have not begun to live, but the time is drawing near. Already, thousands are using this great power, and thousands are eagerly watching and waiting for the new day.

WHY BELIEF IS NECESSARY

❖ ❖ ❖

When we pray, we must always believe. Our idea of prayer is not asking God for things that we need. As we have said before, this already-believing is necessary because all is mind, and until we have provided that full acceptance, we have not made a mold into which mind could pour itself and through which it could manifest. This positive belief is absolutely essential to real creative work, and if we do not have it yet, then we must develop it.

All is law, and cause and effect obtain through all life. Mind is cause, and what we call *matter*, or the visible, is effect. As water will freeze into the form that it is poured, so mind will solidify into the forms that our thoughts take. Thought is form. We as individuals provide the form; we never create. There is something that does all this for us. Our sole activity is the use of this power. This power is always at hand, ready to be spoken into and at once ready to move the words into visible expression. But the mold that most of us provide is a very poor one, and we change it so quickly that it is more like a motion picture than anything else.

Already we have the power. It is the gift of the Most High in its finite expression. Our ignorance of its use has cursed us to create the wrong form, which in its turn has caused mind to produce the form that we have thought into it. We can never hope to escape from this law of cause and effect. While we may think of it as difficult at first, when we understand, we will see it as absolute justice without which there could be no real, self-acting individual life at all. Because of our divine individuality, even God may have to await our recognition of God and God's laws.

People in business will do well to remember this and form their thought so that they will receive what they send out. No thought of discouragement or disorder should ever be created, but only positive assurance, strong thoughts of success, of divine activity, the feeling that with God all things are possible, and the belief that we are one with that great mind. These are the thoughts that make for success.

The realization that we are dealing with one and not two powers enables us to think with clearness. We are not troubled about competition, opposition, or failure, because there is nothing but life, and this life is constantly giving to us all that we could ask for, wish, or think into it.

We can now see how essential it is that thought should be focused and that we should think always and only about what we want, never letting our mind dwell on anything else. In this way, the Spirit works through us.

WHERE SO MANY FAIL

✦　✦　✦

Ordinary people, sitting down to pray about their business, unconsciously do the thing that they should avoid, and then they wonder why they did not get the desired results. Most people simply sit and wish for something. They might have a great desire or hope for it. They may even go so far as to believe that their desire is going to happen. All this is good as far as it goes, but it does not go far enough. What we must do is provide that already-having-received attitude. This may seem difficult at first, but we can easily see that it is necessary, and since it is the only way that mind works, this is what we must do.

Power *is*, and mind *is*, and life *is*, but they have to flow through us in order to express in our lives. We are dealing with law, and nature must be obeyed before it will work for us. Just realize that this law is as natural a law as any other of God's laws and use it with the same intelligence that you would use the law of electricity, and then you will get the desired results. We provide the thought form around which the divine energies play and to which they attract the conditions necessary for the fulfillment of the thought.

This all that we have to do when we pray. We have to clear our minds of all fear, of every sense of separation from the divine mind. Law is, but we must enforce it, or use it, in our own lives. Nothing can happen to us that is not first an accepted belief in our own consciousness. We may not always be aware of what is going on within, but practice will enable us to control our thought more and more so that we will be able to think what we want to think, regardless of what may seem to be the case.

All people have within themselves the capacity of knowing and making use of the law, but it must be consciously developed. This is done by practice and the willingness to learn and utilize what we know.

The individual who has the most power is the one who has the greatest realization of the divine presence and to whom this means the most as an active principle of life.

We all need more backbone and less wishbone. There

is something that waits only for our recognition to spring into being, bringing with it all the power in the universe.

USING THE IMAGINATION

✦ ✦ ✦

Imagine yourself surrounded by a mind so plastic and so receptive that it receives the slightest impression of your thought. Whatever you think, it takes up and executes for you. Every thought is received and acted on. Not some, but all thoughts. Whatever the pattern you provide, that will be your demonstration. If you cannot get over thinking that you are poor, then you will remain poor. As soon as you become rich in your thought, you will be rich in your expression. These are not mere words, but the deepest truth that has ever come to the human race. Hundreds of thousands of the most intelligent thinkers and the most spiritual people today are proving this truth. You are not dealing with illusions, but with realities. Pay no more attention to those who ridicule these ideas than you would to the blowing of the wind.

In the center of your own soul, choose what you want to become, what you want to accomplish, then keep it to yourself. Every day, in the silence of absolute conviction, know that it is now done. As far you are concerned, it is just as much done as it will be when you experience it in the outer. Imagine yourself to be what you want to be. See only that which you desire, and refuse even to think of the other. Stick to it, and never doubt. Say many times a day, "I am that thing." The great universal power of mind is that thing, and it cannot fail.

Our Right of Choice

❖ ❖ ❖

We are created as individuals, and as such, we have the power of choice. Many people seem to think that we should not choose, that since we have asked the Spirit to lead us, we no longer need to act or choose. Though this is taught by many teachers, it is not consistent with our individuality. Unless we had this privilege, this power of choice, we would not be individuals. We need to learn that Spirit can choose through us. But when this happens, it is an act on our part. Even though we say, "I will not choose," we are still choosing, because we are choosing not to choose.

We cannot escape the fact that we are made in such a way that every step life is a constant choice. We need to select what we feel to be right and know that the universe will never deny us anything. We choose; mind creates. We should endeavor to choose that which will always express a greater life, and we must remember that the Spirit is always seeking to express love and beauty through us. If we are attuned to these facts and are working in harmony with the great creative power, we do not need to doubt its willingness to work for us.

We must know exactly what it is that we wish get the perfect mental picture of. We must absolutely believe that we now have it and never do or say anything that denies it.

Old Age and Opportunity

❖ ❖ ❖

One of our errors is the belief that we are too old to do things. This comes from a lack of understanding what life really is. Life is consciousness, not years. A seventy-year-old person should be better able to demonstrate than the one who is twenty. This older person should have evolved a higher thought, and it is thought and not conditions that we are dealing with.

Amelia Barr was fifty-three before she wrote a book. After that, she wrote over eighty, all of which had a large circulation. Mary Baker Eddy was sixty before she began her work, and she attended to all of her great activities until she passed away from this plane to a higher one. I once worked with a man who was over sixty, one who thought his chance for success had gone, and through teaching him these principles, in a year's time he became a prosperous business person. He is now doing well and was never before so happy in his life. The last time I met him, he said that business was increasing daily. Each day, he stands in his store and claims more activity. He speaks the word and realizes increase all the time.

If this were not possible, then life would not be worth living. What are a few years in eternity? We must get over false notions about age and competition. In the truth, the word *competition* is never mentioned. The people who think about it have never known the truth.

Life is what we make it from within and never from without. We are just as old as we think we are, no matter what the number of years may have been that we have lived on this planet.

Demonstrating Success in Business

❖   ❖   ❖

All demonstrations take place within ourselves. Creation is eternally flowing through all things. The law is always working from that inner pattern. We do not struggle with conditions; we use principles that create conditions. What we can mentally encompass, we can accomplish, no matter how hard it may seem from the outside.

All external things are but the outer rim of inner thought activity. You can easily prove this for yourself. If you are in business running an ice cream stand and are not doing good business, look carefully into your own thought and see what you will find. You will find you have an established a belief there that business is not good. You are not feeling a sense of activity. You will not find within your thought any feeling of success. You are not expecting many customers.

Some may say, "What is the matter? Why are you not doing more business?" Your answer might be, "People don't seem to want what I have to sell" or "I am too old to compete with modern methods," or even "Times are hard." All this is negative thought.

You should not believe a negative word of this. Causation is in mind and not in matter. The whole thing is in your own mind. The real trouble is that you don't feel that you are a success.

All is mind. Nothing moves unless mind moves it, and you are a center in this mind. Your thought decides whether your business will be a success or a failure. Does this mean you want to fail? Of course you do not, yet while you wish success, you are thinking failure and fearing it. There is a law that makes your thought, never asking questions, but at once setting about its fulfillment. How can this be? Well, how did anything come into being? There was a time when nothing existed except Spirit, so whatever has come into being must have come from that Spirit, because what we see must come from that which we do not see. Logically, then, what you do not see must be the cause of everything, and that cause works by law, which, being everywhere, must be in you. Without knowing where your thought processes were leading, you must concede that you yourself are the reason for what happens in your life, be it success or failure. God couldn't make you any other way without making you a self-choosing individual. This is plain.

So what are you going to do about it? For every time that you have thought failure, you are going to replace it with strong, radiant thoughts of success. You are going to speak activity into your business. You are going to see nothing but activity and to know that it is law that you are using, universal law, and as such, your thought is as sure as the thought of God.

Daily, you are going to give to the great creative mind exactly what you want to have happen. You will see only what you desire, and in the silence of your soul, you will speak, and it will be done unto you. You will come to believe that a great divine love flows through you and your affairs. You will be grateful for this love. It fills your life. It satisfies your soul. You are a different person. You are so filled with activity and courage that when you meet people, they will wonder at your energy. They will begin to want to come in contact with you. They will feel uplifted.

In the course of a few months, you will be a success. People will come to you and say, "How do you do it?" The answer will be the same that was given to you a few months ago.

Always remember this. Life is from within outward and never from without inward. You are the center of power in your life.

Do not take on false suggestions. The world is full of calamity howlers. Turn from them, every one, no matter how great you think they may be. You don't have time to waste over anything that is negative. You are a success, and you are giving to the law every day just what you want done, and the law is always working for you. All fear has gone, and you know that there is only one power in the universe. Happy is the one who knows this the greatest of all truths.

The whole thing resolves itself into our mental ability to control our thought. Those who do this can have what they want, do what they wish, and become what they will. Life, God, the universe, is yours.

MONEY AS A SPIRITUAL IDEA

❖   ❖   ❖

Many people think that money must be evil, although I have never as yet met anyone who did not want a lot of this evil in their lives!

If everything is an expression of life, then money is also an expression of life and, as such, must be good. Without a certain amount of money in this world, we would have a hard time. But how do we acquire wealth? Money doesn't make itself, so not being self-creative, it must be an effect. Behind money must be the cause that projects it. That cause is never seen, because no cause is ever seen. Consciousness is cause, and people who have a money consciousness have the outward expression of it. People who don't have this mental likeness, won't.

We need to acquire a money consciousness. This may seem very material, but the true idea of money is not material. It is spiritual. We need to make our unity with it. We can never do this when we keep it away from us by thinking that we do not have it. We change the method and begin to make our unity with supply by declaring that all the power in the universe is daily bringing to us all that we can use. We feel the presence of supply and know that it is ours now.

When you feel that you now have it, it will be given to you. Work with yourself until there is nothing in you that doubts. Money can not be kept away from those who understand that everything is mind and that divine law governs their lives.

Give thanks for perfect supply each day. Feel that it is yours, that you have entered into the full possession of it now.

Refuse to talk about poverty or limitation. Persist in the thought that you are rich, Get the million-dollar consciousness. This will react into everything that you do.

See money coming to you from every source and from every direction. Know that everything is working for your good.

Realize in your life the presence of the omnipotent power. Speak forth into it and feel it respond to your approach.

Whenever you see anything or anybody whom you think has more than you, immediately affirm that you have the same thing. This does not mean that you take theirs, but that you have as just much. It means that all you need is yours.

Whenever you think about anything big, at once say, "That means me." In this way you learn to unify yourself in the law with large concepts, and according to the way that law works, it will tend to produce that thing for you.

Never let yourself doubt for even a minute. Always be positive about yourself. Keep watch over the inner workings of your thought, and the law will do the rest.

ACTION

❖   ❖   ❖

The universe is teeming with activity. There is motion everywhere. Nothing ever stands still. All activity comes from mind. If we want to be in line with things, we must move. This doesn't mean that we must strain or struggle, but we must be willing to do our part by letting the law work through us.

God can do for us only as we will allow God to do through us. Intelligence gives us some ideas, and in our turn, we work on them. But our work is no longer done with a sense of doubt or fear, because we know that we are dealing with something that never makes a mistake. We proceed with a calm confidence born of the inner trust in a power that is infinite. Behind all our movements, then, is a great purpose—to let the law work through us.

The law of activity must be complied with. We must be willing to take the way of outer activity. Jesus went to the tomb of Lazarus. We may have to go, but there will accompany us something that never fails.

We must use the law of activity in our business. So many business places have such an atmosphere of inactivity and produce such dull feelings that we at once lose all interest in what is going on there. We don't feel like buying anything. We leave those places without any apparent reason and go to another where we feel that all is life and motion, all is activity. We feel confident that this is the place we were looking for. We will buy here. We find just what we want. We are satisfied with our purchase and go away cheerful.

To create this activity, something more than thought is essential. Thought does come first, but those who have this thought of activity will naturally manifest it in vigorous, energetic movements that help to produce a spirit of activity in their business and in everything they undertake. Wherever you see a person who does not move, you will find someone whose thought is inactive. The two always go together.

Store or business owners should always be moving their goods. They should always be doing something. People will see this and, feeling the thought of activity behind it, want to buy there. We are not attracted to a store that always has the same thing on the same shelf. The world likes action, change. Action is life.

If store clerks start to think activity and begin to manifest it even though they may not be waiting on customers, in a short time they will be. Alertness is the word. Always be alert. There must be mental alertness before there can be any physical activity.

Act as though things are happening even though they may not appear to be. Keep things moving, and soon you will have to avoid the rush. Activity is genius. Half the stores that you go into make you sleepy before you get out, and you feel as though you can't get out fast enough. The other half are alive, and those are the ones doing the business of the world.

Those who are active in their thoughts don't have to sit by themselves to think. They work while they think and, thus, comply with the law, which has to work through them. The thought of activity makes them move, the thought of confidence makes their movements sure, and the thought of supreme guidance makes their work intelligent.

You must be careful to not get into a rut. Always be doing something new and different, and then you will find that life becomes a great game in which you are taking the leading part.

Life will never be tiresome to the active mind and body. It becomes so interesting that we wonder if we will ever get enough of it. Some people get into such lazy mental habits that a new idea cannot find entrance. Great things are done by people who think great thoughts and then go out into the world to make their dreams come true.

If you can't find anything new to do, go home and rearrange your room or move the furniture around. Eat dinner outside. It will start something moving and changing in you that will never stop. Wide awake people can find so many things to do that they don't even have time to begin in this life. They know that eternity is necessary to carry out the ideas that they have already evolved.

Everything comes from mind, but mind acts on itself, and we must act on ourselves and on conditions, not as a slave, but as a master. Be interested in life if you want life to be interested in you. Act in life, and life will act through you. You will become one of the great people on Earth.

IDEAS OF THE INFINITE

❖   ❖   ❖

Suppose that you wish to draw from the universal mind
some definite idea, some guidance, some information,
some direction. How are you going to do this? First, you
must become convinced that you can do it.

Where do all the inventions come from? Where did
Edison get his information about electricity? Where, if
not directly from the mind of the universe? Everything
that has ever come into the human race comes directly
from mind. There is nowhere else it could come from.

Every invention is only a discovery of something
that already is, although we may not have seen it before.
Where does the harmony of music come from? Where
could it originate except in mind? Great musicians listen

and hear something that we do not hear. Their ears are attuned to harmony. They catch it straight from life itself and interpret it to the world. We are surrounded by the music of the spheres, but few of us catch the sound.

We are so filled with worry that the divine melody is never heard. If we could see, if we could hear, if we could understand, if we only realized the presence of the all, we could do anything.

When a great thought springs up in the mind of an individual, when a great poem is written, when a great work of art is wrought by some receptive artist, it is simply a sign that the veil is thin between, and this person has caught a glimpse of reality.

For most of us, inspiration is not to be depended on. We must take the slower but surer method of receiving directly from the Infinite. The method for knowing how to achieve something or begin a certain line of action is simple and effective.

First, you must be quiet within yourself. You must not be confused by any outward appearance. Never become disturbed by effects. They didn't make themselves and have no intelligence to contradict you.

Be quiet until you realize the presence of absolute intelligence all around you, of the mind that knows. Now, get a perfect picture of just what you desire. You cannot get a picture unless you know what it is you want. Put your mind in touch with universal mind, saying exactly what you are waiting for. Ask for it, believe that you are receiving it, and wait. After a few minutes, declare that you know *now*. Even though you may not seem to know, you have received the impression in the depths of consciousness. Give thanks that you now receive. Do this every day until you get some direction. It is sometimes a good thing to do this just before going to sleep.

After you have done this, never deny the knowledge that has been given you. The time will come when some idea will begin to take form. Wait for it, and when it does appear, act on it with all the conviction of one who is perfectly sure of oneself.

You have received understanding directly from the source of all understanding and knowledge from the source of knowledge. Anyone can do this if they will be persistent. It is a sure direction and guidance that will never fail us. But we must be sure that we are not denying in other moments that which we affirm in the moments of faith. In this way, we will make fewer mistakes, and in time our lives will be controlled by supreme wisdom and understanding.

Don't Be a Leaner

❖   ❖   ❖

Never lean on other people. You have your own strength, which is great enough to do all that is necessary. The Almighty has implanted genius within the soul of everyone, and we need to unearth that inner genius and cause it to shine forth. We will never do this while we look to others for guidance. "To thine own self repair, wait thou within the silence dim, and thou shalt find God there."

All the power and intelligence of the universe is already within, waiting to be utilized. The divine spark must be fanned into a blaze of the living fire of your own divinity.

Self-reliance is the word to dwell on. Listen to your

own voice. It will speak in terms that are unmistakable. Trust in your own self more than in all else. All great people have learned to do this. Every one of us, within our own souls, is in direct communication with the infinite understanding. When we depend on other people, we are simply taking their light and trying to light our path with it. When we depend on ourselves, we are depending on that inner voice that is God speaking in and through us. "We are the inlet and the outlet to all there is in God." God has made us and brought us up to where we recognize our own individuality. From now on, we will have to let God express through us. If we were different, we would not be individuals. "Behold, I stand at the door and knock." This is a statement of the near presence of power; but we, the individual, must open the door. This door is our thought, and we are the guardians of it. When we do open the door, we will find that the divine presence is right at hand, waiting, ready, and willing to do for us all that we can believe.

We are strong with the strength of the Infinite. We are not weak. We are great and not small. We are one with the infinite mind.

When you have a real thing to do, keep it to yourself. Don't talk about it. Just know in your own mind what it is you want and keep still about it. Often when we think that we will do some big thing, we begin to talk about it, and the first thing we know is that all the power seems to be gone.

We all send out into mind a constant stream of thought. The clearer it is, the better it will manifest. If it becomes doubtful, it will not have a clear manifestation. If it is confused, it will manifest only confusion. All this is according to the law of cause and effect, and we cannot change that law. Too often, when we tell our friends what we are going to do, they confuse our thoughts by laughing about it or doubting our capacity to do so large a thing. This would not happen if we were always positive, but when we become the least bit negative, we may react and lose the power of clearness that is absolutely necessary to good creative work.

When you want to do a big thing, get the mental pattern. Make it perfect, know just what it means, enlarge your thought, keep it to yourself, pass it over to the creative power behind all things, wait and listen, and when the impression comes, follow it with assurance. Don't talk to anyone about it, and you will succeed where all others fail.

CAUSES AND CONDITIONS

❖   ❖   ❖

When we realize that life is not fundamentally physical, but mental and spiritual, it will be easy to see that we can demonstrate what we want by a certain mental and spiritual process.

We are not dealing with conditions, but with causes. Causes originate only from the unseen side of life. This is not strange, because the same can be said of electricity, or even of life itself. We do not see life; we see what it does. This we call a condition. Of itself, it is simply an effect. We are living in the outer world of effects and the inner world of causes. We set these causes in motion by our thought, and through the power inherent within the cause, we express the thought as a condition. It follows that the cause must be equal to the effect and that the effect always evaluates with the cause held in mind. Everything comes from one substance, and our thought qualifies that substance and determines what is to take place in our life.

The whole teaching of the *Bhagavad-Gita* is that there is only oneness, and that oneness becomes to us just what we first believe into it. In other words, we manifest the unmanifested. This in no way takes away from the omnipotence of God, but adds to it, because God has created something that is able to do this. God still rules the universe, but we are given the power to rule our lives.

We must realize, then, that we are absolutely dealing with a substance that we have a right to deal with, and by learning its laws, we will be able to subject them to our use, just as Edison did with electricity. Law is, but we must use it.

The substance that we deal with is never limited, but we often are because we draw only what we believe.

Our being limited is no reason why the universe should have limitation. Our limitation is only our unbelief. Life can give us a big thing or a little thing. When it gives us a little thing, it is not limited any more than life is limited when it makes a grain of sand, because it could just as well have made a planet. In the great scheme of things, all kinds of forms, both small and large, are necessary, which when combined make the complete whole. The power and substance behind everything remain infinite.

This life can only come to us through us, and that becoming is the passing of Spirit into expression in our lives through the form of the thought that we give to it. In itself, life is never limited. An ant has just as much life as an elephant, though smaller in size. The question is not one of size, but of consciousness.

We are not limited by actual boundaries, but by false ideas about life and by a failure to recognize that we are dealing with the infinite.

Limitation is an experience of the human race, but it is not the fault of God. It is the fault of humankind's perception. To prove this, when anyone breaks the bonds of the false sense of life, they at once begin to express less and less limitation. It is a matter of the growth of the inner idea.

When told this, some people say, "Do you think that I decided to be poor and miserable? Do you take me for a fool?" No, you are not a fool, but it is quite possible that you have been fooled. Most of us have been. I know of no one who has escaped being fooled about life. You may not have had thoughts of poverty, but at the same time, you may have had thoughts that produced it. Just watch the process of your thinking and see how many times a day you think about something you would not want to happen. This will satisfy you that you need to be watchful and that your thought needs to be controlled.

We need to reverse the process of our thinking and see to it that we think only positive, constructive thoughts. A calm determination to think just what we want to think, regardless of conditions, will do much to put us on the highway to a greater realization of life.

Of course, the road is not easy, but we will be growing. Daily, we will be giving to the creative mind a newer and greater concept to be worked out into the life around us. Daily, we will be overcoming some negative tendency. We must stick to it until we gain the mastery of all our thought, and in that day, we will rise never to fall again.

You must be good-natured with yourself, never becoming discouraged or giving up until you overcome. Feel that you are always backed by an omnipotent power and a kind Spirit of love, and the way will be become easier.

Mental Equivalents

❖   ❖   ❖

We cannot demonstrate life beyond our mental ability to embody. We give birth to an idea only from within ourselves. We put into our thinking that which we are. What we are not, we cannot put into it.

If we are to draw from life what we want, we must first think into life, because life always produces what we think. In order to have success, we must first conceive it in our thought. This is not because we are creators, but because the flow of life into manifestation through us must take the form we give to it, and if we want a thing, we must have within ourselves the mental equivalent before we get it.

This is what Jesus meant when he said that we must

believe when we pray. This belief is providing within us something that knows before it sees what it asks for.

For instance, suppose we are praying for activity in our affairs. (Keep in mind, our idea of prayer is the accepting of a thing before we get it.) Before this activity can come, we must have it within ourselves. We must come to see activity in everything. There must be something that corresponds to the thing that we want. We must have a mental equivalent.

We find that we attract to ourselves as much of anything we embody within. As water will reach only its own level, so our outward conditions will only reproduce our inner realizations.

We will always attract to ourselves exactly what we are. But we can learn to provide within the image of what we desire and, in a definite way, use the law to get just what we need. If at first we do not have a great realization of activity, we will have to work on what we do have. Since our outer conditions come up to meet the inner cause, it will be much easier to enlarge the inner receptivity for something greater and more worthwhile. We must all start somewhere, and that somewhere is within ourselves. We must make the affirmation within, and there, too, we must do the real work of realization. At first, the way may seem difficult because we are constantly confronted with that which seems to be, and we are not always sure of ourselves or strong enough to over-come. We may rest content in the assurance that we are growing. Every day, we provide a bigger concept of life. With inner growth, we will have an enlarged power to speak forth into the creative mind, with the result that we will get a fresh impulse and be doing a bigger thing for ourselves. Growth and realization are always from within and never from without.

The old race suggestion of fear, poverty, and limitation must be done away with, and we must clear our thought daily from all that limits the one from showing forth in our life.

Remember that we are dealing with one power, not two. This will make it easier because we do not have to overcome any condition. Conditions flow in from with-out, not from without in.

If we were to move to a new town, we would at once begin to attract to us just what we bring to our thought. We should be very careful what we think. We should know just what we want and daily give it over to the supreme mind, knowing that it will work for us. Old thoughts must be destroyed, and new ones must take their places. Every time the old thought comes, look it squarely in the face and declare that it has no part in your mind. It has no power over you. You state the law and rely on it to the exclusion of all else. Daily, try to see and understand more. Feel every day that you are being especially looked after. There is no special creation for any individual. We all specialize the law every time we think into it, because all our thought is accepted and acted on.

A good practice is to sit and realize that you are a center of divine attraction, that all things are coming to you, and that the power within is going out and drawing back all that you will ever need. Don't argue with it, just do it, and when you have finished, leave it all to the law, knowing that it will be done. Declare that all life, all love and power is now in your life. Declare that you are now in the midst of plenty. Stick to it even though you may not as yet see the result. It will work, and those who believe the most always get the most. Think of the law as your friend, always looking out for your interest. Trust in it completely, and it will bring your good to you.

ONE LAW AND MANY MANIFESTATIONS

❖   ❖   ❖

People often ask if the law can bring harm as well as good. This question would never be asked if people understood what universal law really means. It will bring us what we think. All law will do the same thing. The law of electricity will either light our house or burn it down. We decide what we are to do with the law. Law is always impersonal. There is no likelihood of using the law for harmful purposes if we always use it for the more complete expression.

We must not use law for any purpose that we would not like to experience ourselves. This should answer all our questions of that nature. Do I really want the thing I ask for? Am I willing to take for myself what I ask for other people? How can we use the law for evil if we desire only good? We cannot, and we should not bother about it. We want only good for ourselves and for the whole world.

When we have started causation, the law will at once set to work carrying out our plans. Never distrust the law or become afraid, otherwise you might misuse it. This is a great mistake. All law is impersonal and does not care who uses it. It will bring to all of us exactly what is already in our thought. We cannot use it in a destructive way for long, because it will destroy us if we persist in using it wrongly. We have no responsibility for anyone except ourselves. Get over all ideas that you must save the world. We have tried that and failed. We may, by demonstrating in our own lives, prove that the law really exists as the great power behind all things. This is all that we can do. We must each do the same thing for ourselves. Let the dead bury their dead, and see that you live. In this, you are not selfish, but are simply proving that law governs your life. All can do the same when they come to believe, and none until they believe.

TRANSCENDING PREVIOUS CONDITIONS

❖ ❖ ❖

What if we attract something that we do not want? What about all the things that we have already attracted into our lives? Must we still suffer until the last penalty is paid? Are we bound by karma? Yes, in a certain degree we are bound by what we have done. It is impossible to set law in motion and not have it produce. What we sow, we must also reap, of that there is no doubt. But the Bible also says that if we repent, our "sins are blotted out and remembered no more forever." Here we have two statements that seem not to agree. The first says that we must suffer from what we have done, and the second says that under certain conditions, we will not have to suffer. What are those conditions? A changed attitude toward the law! It means that we must stop thinking and acting in the wrong way.

When we do this, we are taken out of the old order and established in the new. Some may say, "If that is true, what about the law of cause and effect? Is that broken?" No, the law is not broken. It still works even if we continued to use it the wrong way. But when we reverse the cause, that is, think and act in a different way, then we have changed the flow of the law.

It is still the same law, but we have changed its flow so that instead of limiting us and punishing us, it frees and blesses. It is still the law, but we have changed our attitude toward it. We might throw a ball at the window, and if nothing stopped it, it would break the glass. Here is law in motion. But if someone catches the ball before it reaches the window, the glass will not be broken. The flow of law will be changed, that is all. So can we. No matter what has happened in the past, we can transcend the old experience so that it will no longer have any effect on us. If we have attracted something that is not best to keep, we will remember that we do not have to keep it. It was the best that we knew at the time, so was good as far as it went, but now we know more and can do better.

Because law works without variation, so does the law of attraction work the same way. All that we have to do is to drop the undesired thing from our thought, forgive ourselves, and start anew. We must never even think of it again. Let go of it once and for all. Our various experiences will teach us more and more to mold all of our thoughts and desires so that they will be in line with the fundamental purpose of the great mind, the expression of that which is perfect. To fear to make conscious use of the law would be to paralyze all efforts of progress.

More and more, will we come to see that a great cosmic plan is being worked out and that all we have to do is to lend ourselves to it in order for us to attain a real degree of life. As we subject our thought to the greater purposes, we are correspondingly blessed, because we are working more in line with the Spirit who knew the end from the beginning. We should never lose sight of the fact that we are each given the individual right to use the law, and we cannot escape from using it.

We then go forward with the belief that a greater power is working through us, that all law is a law of good, that we have planted our seed of thought in the mind of the absolute, and that we can go our way rejoicing in the divine privilege of working with the Infinite.

UNDERSTANDING AND
MISUNDERSTANDING

❖   ❖   ❖

Some people are constantly unhappy because they seem always to be misunderstood. They find it hard to use the law of attraction in an affirmative way and keep on drawing to themselves experiences that they could have avoided. The trouble with them is that they have an undercurrent of thought that neutralizes or destroys whatever helpful thoughts they have set in motion in their moments of greater strength. Such people are usually very sensitive, and while this is a quality that is most creative when under control, it is most destructive when uncontrolled, because it is chaotic. These people should first come to know the law and see how it works, and then treat themselves to overcome all sensitiveness. They should realize that everyone in the world is a friend and should prove this by never saying anything unkind to anyone or about anyone. They must within themselves see all people as perfect beings made in the divine image and see nothing else. Then, they will in time be able to say that this is also the way that all people see them. Holding this as the law of their lives, they will destroy all negative thought. With the power that is always in a sensitive person but that is now under control, they will find that life is theirs to do with as they please, the only requirement being that as they sow, so must they also reap. We know that anything that is unlike good is of short duration, but anything that embodies the good is like God, ever present and eternal. We free ourselves through the same law under which we first bound ourselves.

Ordinary individuals unknowingly do things that destroy any possibility of getting good results in their demonstrations of prosperity. They affirm their good and make their unity with it, and this is right. But they do not stop looking at it in others, which is wrong and is the cause of confusion. We cannot affirm a principle and deny it in the same breath. We must become what we want, and we will never be able to do that while we still persist in seeing what we do not want, no matter where we see it. We cannot believe that something is possible for us without believing the same for every individual.

One of the ways of attainment is, of necessity, the way of universal love—coming to see all as true children of God, one with the infinite mind. This is no mere sentiment, but the clear statement of a fundamental law, and those who do not obey it are opposing the very thing that brought them into expression. It is true that, through mental means alone, they may bring themselves things, and they may hold them as long as the will lasts. This is the ordinary way, but we want more compelling things to appear. What we want is that things should gravitate to us, because we are employing the same law that God uses. When we attain this attitude of mind, then that which is brought into manifestation will never be lost, because it will be as eternal as the law of God and cannot be destroyed forever. It is a comfort to know that we do not have to make things happen, only that the law of divine love is all that we ever need. It will relieve the overworked brain and the tired muscle just to be still and know we are one with the all-in-all.

How can we enter in if we are believing for ourselves and, at the same time, beholding the beam in our neighbor's eye? Does that not distract the view and pervert our own natures? We must see only the good and let nothing else enter into our minds. Giving universal love to all people and to all things is only returning love to the source of all love, to the one who creates all in love and holds everything in divine care. The sun shines on all alike. Will we separate and divide that which God has so carefully united? We are dividing our own things when we do this, and sooner or later the law of absolute justice that weighs out to each of us our just measure will balance the account, and then we will be obliged to suffer for the mistakes we have made. God does not bring this agony on us, but we have imposed it on ourselves from selfish motives alone. We must love all things and look on all things as good, made from the substance of the Spirit.

We can only hope to bring to ourselves that which we draw through the avenue of love. We must watch our thinking, and if we have anything against any soul, get rid of it as soon as possible. This is the only safe and sure way. At the supreme moment of sacrifice, Jesus asked that the Lord forgive all the wrong that was being done to him. Do we think we can do it in a better way? If we do not at the present time love all people, then we must learn how to do it, and the way will become easier when all condemnation is gone forever and we behold only good. God is good, and God is love. More than this, we cannot ask or conceive.

Another thing we must eliminate is talking about limitation. We must not even think of or read about it, or have any connection with it in any of our thinking, because we get only that which we think, no more and no less. This will be difficult to do. But if we remember that we are working out the science of our being, though it may seem long and hard at times, we sooner or later do it, and once done, it is done forever. Every step in advance is an eternal step and will never have to be taken again. We are not building for a day or a year, but we are building for all time and for eternity. So we will build the statelier mansion under the supreme wisdom and the unfailing guidance of the Spirit, and we will do to everyone as we would have them do to us. There is no other way. The wise will listen, look, and learn, then follow what they know to be the only way that is in line with the divine will and purpose. So will everyone see that God is good, and in God is no evil.

No Unusual Experience

✦   ✦   ✦

In demonstrating the truth of supply, we do not have to experience any peculiar emotion or psychic experience. We do not need to feel any thrills or anything of that sort. While it is true that some of these things may come, we should remember that what we are doing is dealing with law, and that as law, it will obey us when we comply with its nature and contact it in the right way. What we are doing is stating something into mind, and if the impression is clear in our own minds that it is and that it is done, we have put all the activity we can put into it until such a time as something happens in the external for us to work on.

Some people say, "I wish that I could feel something

when I give a prayer treatment." This is a mistake and is an attempt to give a physical reason for life. What we need to feel is that since God is all and is good, God wants us to have only the good. Feeling this, we should take what is already made for us. Our attitude toward such a good creator should constantly be one of thanksgiving. When we begin to prove the power of the truth, we will always maintain this attitude. Know that you are dealing with a sure thing. All you have to do is to know positively into it and wait for the results to come in the outer. Then, do what your own good sense tells you to do, because this is the thought of God through you. More and more, you will find that you are being led out of difficulty into the freedom that is the divine birthright of every living soul. Go ahead, then, looking only at the things desired and never at the things not wanted. Victory will always be on the side where the majority of your thoughts rest in absolute acceptance.

VISUALIZING

❖　❖　❖

Some people visualize everything that they think of, and many think that it is impossible to make a demonstration unless they possess the power to visualize. This is not the case. While a certain amount of vision is necessary, it must be remembered that we are dealing with a power that is like the soil of the ground that will produce the plant when we plant the seed. It does not matter if we have never before seen a plant like the one that is to be made for us. Our thought is the seed, and mind is the soil.

We are always planting and harvesting. All that we need to do is plant only that which we want to harvest. This is not difficult to understand. We cannot think poverty and at the same time demonstrate plenty. If a person wants to visualize, they may do so, and if they see themselves in full possession of their desire and know that they are receiving, they will make their demonstration. If, on the other hand, they do not visualize, then let them simply state what they want and absolutely believe that they have it, and the result will always be the same.

Remember that you are always dealing with law, and that this is the only way that anything could come into existence. Don't argue over it. That means that you have not as yet become convinced of the truth, otherwise you would not argue. Be convinced, and rest in peace.

WHERE DEMONSTRATION TAKES PLACE

◆　◆　◆

Does demonstration take place in the person for whom we are praying, the practitioner who is praying, or in the mind of God? We are in the mind of God, and so it must take place there. But the recipient of our prayer work is also in the mind of God, otherwise there would be two minds. So it must take place in the mind of the person for whom we are praying also. But that person, too, is the mind of God, so what does it matter where it takes place?

We do not have to project our thought, because mind is right at hand and never leaves us at any time. All that we have to do is to know within ourselves, and when we are absolutely convinced, we will have made the demonstration.

As far as prayer practitioners are concerned, all that they have to do is to convince themselves. Here, their work begins and ends. There is a power that will look after the rest. This is the supreme attitude of faith in higher power. The more faith that we have, the easier it will be for us and the quicker we will receive an answer to our prayer. If we have a simple, childlike faith, it will produce, but it should give us a greater faith when we know something of the way that the law operates. It follows, then, that we should, by understanding, have so great a faith that we will never fail to get the affirmative answer to all our thoughts. Each victory will strengthen us until the time comes when we will no longer have to say "I hope or believe," but "I know."

Part 2

Practice

❖   ❖   ❖

Prayer Treatments

◆　◆　◆

The way to give a prayer treatment is, first of all, to absolutely believe that you can. Believe that your word goes forth into a real creative power that at once takes it up and begins to operate on it. Feel that all things are possible to this power. It knows nothing but its own power to do that which it wishes to do. It receives the impress of your thought and acts on it.

It is never safe to pray for anything that you do not wish to happen. This means that what you would want for another, you must be at first willing to receive yourself.

Believe that your word is to be acted on by an almighty power. Feel its great reality in and through all things you speak into it, and declare exactly what you wish it to do for you, never doubting in your own mind that it will do just as you have directed.

All that prayer practitioners have to do is to convince themselves—to know, to believe—and that which they state will happen to them. One of the first things, then, is to be definite, to have a mental likeness of the thing that you desire, to know exactly what you want. This mental likeness, this absolute acceptance of the fact that it now is, must never be overlooked. Without it, you will not accomplish.

We sit down with our own souls, at peace with the world, at peace with ourselves. We realize that we are dealing with something that is a reality, something that cannot fail. We try to get a clear concept of the thing. We rest in that realization, and the universal creative power takes it up and acts on it.

We have stated exactly what we wanted done to us. We have believed. We have believed that we have received. Never again will we contradict the fact that we have stated. The person who can do this is sure of getting results.

Understanding and Guidance

❖ ❖ ❖

The inner person is always in immediate connection with the infinite of understanding. We are immersed in a living intelligence. We are surrounded by a power that knows, because "in Spirit, we live and move and have our being."

If our outer thought was never confused, we would at all times draw from this infinite source of knowledge. We would be guided by it and never make mistakes. Our minds would be like the smooth surface of a lake, unruffled by wind or storm.

But with most of us, this is not the case. We become confused in the outer, so that the surface of the mind is in turmoil, no longer clear and transparent, and we cannot get the clear vision, the real guidance. We get things wrong because we do not see clearly.

The development of understanding is learning to draw from the infinite understanding. We can never do this while we are confused in our thinking.

The first thing to do when we wish a greater understanding is to be still and listen to the inner voice, to withdraw for a few moments into the silence of the soul, taking here what we already know and realizing that a greater intelligence is enlarging it.

Here, we indefinitely take the pattern of our thought, the thing that we are working on, and ask for and receive new light. We hold this up in the divine light and try to believe that we are being guided. We state that supreme intelligence and absolute power are acting on our thought and bringing it to pass. It is now guiding us, and we will make no mistake. We hold ourselves in the secret place of the Most High and abide under the shadow of the Almighty.

How to Know Just What to Do

❖   ❖   ❖

We often find ourselves confronted by the problem of how to begin. We are not sure what we want to do. We see no way to begin anything and see nothing to begin on. When we find ourselves in this position, humanly speaking, not knowing where to turn, then of all times we must be quiet and listen. Then, we must know that the same power that started all things will also start us on the right road, because without some superior power, we will surely fail.

People in the business world often find themselves in this position. They realize that something must be done, but they do not know how get the idea to work out.

At those times, we must wait and know that the same

power that first thought a universe into being can also think our world and work into being. It knows all things. It knows how to begin, and it cannot fail. We wish in some way to connect with this power that will never fail us so that we may draw from it some idea to begin with.

We must realize that there is something that waits for the idea before it responds and makes manifest in this realization. It may not come at first, but we must be patient, never doubting. Waiting in faith, it will come.

I once knew a man in business who was connected with a firm that had always been very successful. But something had occurred that was causing to him to lose traction. This had been going on for a year, and things were going from bad to worse. Failure seemed inevitable. Then, he became interested in spiritual philosophy. He was told he could draw an idea from the infinite and work it out on the plane of the visible. He told his partners that he wished to go home for a few days, and that when he came back, he would have worked out an idea that would put the business on a successful track. They laughed at him, as people generally laugh at something they do not understand, but having no other plan, they gave their consent. He went home for three days and sat in deep thought, claiming supreme guidance and absolute leading of the Spirit. During this time, a complete plan formed in his mind as to the exact method to pursue in the business. He returned and told his plan to his partners. Again they laughed, saying it could not be done and that it would not work. But again they consented, knowing it was this or failure.

He then went to work carrying out all the details of his thought, following each leading that had come to him during those three days, and within a year he brought the failing business to a standard that transcended anything they had ever experienced. He proved the law and became such an expert that he gave up his business and devoted his entire time to helping other people to do the same for themselves.

What this individual did, anyone can do who will follow the same course and refuse to become discouraged. There is a power that simply waits for our recognition of it in order for it to spring into our thought as an unfailing leading, an unerring guidance. To those who lean on the ever-outstretched arm of the infinite, life is big with limitless possibilities.

We must wait and listen, and then go about our outer business with an inner conviction that we are being led into a more perfect expression of life. Everyone can do this.

Following Up a Thought

❖　❖　❖

When we feel that we have the correct leading, when that something inside us tells us that we are led, then no matter what it appears like, we must follow it through. Something beyond our intelligence is doing the thing through us, and we must do nothing to contradict it.

Perhaps it will cause us to do something that seems to go contrary to the experience of the human race. This makes no difference. All advances in invention or along any line have always gone ahead of what the experience of the human race thinks is possible.

Great people are those who get a vision and then go to work to make it come true, never looking with focus and calm determination to one side, but only to the thing until it is accomplished.

It may take much patience and a great deal of faith, but the end is as sure as is the reality of a supreme being itself.

Never hesitate to trust in that inner understanding. Never fear, because it will be right. We are all in the middle of supreme intelligence. It presses against the doors of our thought, waiting to be known. We must be open to it at all times, ready to receive direction and to be guided into greater truths.

THE SINGLE STREAM OF THOUGHT

❖   ❖   ❖

We are all in mind, and what we think into it is taken up and done to us. As we think, it will be done. We cannot think one way today and change our thought the next, and still hope to get the desired results. We must be very clear in our thought, sending out only such thoughts as we wish to see manifested in our condition.

Here is something worth remembering. Unless we are working with people who think as we do, we are better working alone. One stream of thought, even though it may not be powerful, will do more for us than many powerful streams that are at variance with each other. This means that unless we are sure that we are working with people who harmonize, we would do better to work alone. Of course, we cannot retire from business simply because people do not agree with us, but we can keep our thoughts to ourselves. We do not have to leave the world in order to control our thought, but we do have to learn that we can stay in the world and still think exactly what we want to think, regardless of what others are thinking.

One single stream of thought, daily sent into creative mind, will do wonders. Within a year, those who will practice this will have completely changed the conditions of their lives.

The way to practice this is to spend some time daily in thinking and in mentally seeing just what is wanted. See the thing you wish, and then affirm that it is now done. Try to feel that what has been stated is the truth.

Words and affirmations simply give shape to thought; they are not creative. Feeling is creative, and the more feeling that is put into the word, the greater the power it will have over conditions. In doing this, we think of the condition only as an effect, something that follows what we think. It cannot help following our thought. This is the way that all creation comes into expression.

It is a great help to mentally realize that at all times a great stream of thought and power is operating through us. It is constantly going out into mind, where it is taken up and acted on. Our business is to keep that stream of thought just where we want it to be and to be ready at any time to act when the impulse comes into action. Our action must never be negative. It must always be affirmative, because we are dealing with something that cannot fail. We may fail to realize, but the power in itself is infinite and cannot fail.

We are setting in motion, in the absolute a stream of thought, that which will never cease until it accomplishes its purpose. Try to feel this. Be filled with a great joy as you feel that it is given to you to use this great and only power.

Keep the thought clear, and never worry about the way that things seem to be going. Let go of all outer conditions when working in mind, because that is where things are made, that is where creation is going on, and it is now making something for you. This must be believed as never believed before. It must be known as the great reality. It must be felt as the only presence. There is no other way to obtain.

The infinite wants to give, yet we must take, and as far as we are concerned, that taking is mental. Though people may laugh at this, it does not matter. "The one laughs best who laughs last." We know what we believe, and that will be sufficient.

Enlarging Your Thought

❖   ❖   ❖

We can never stand still in our thought. Either we will be growing or we will be going backward. As we can attract to ourselves only what we first have a mental likeness of, it follows that if we wish to attract larger things, we must provide larger thoughts. This enlarging of consciousness is so necessary that too much cannot be said about it.

Most people make only a bit of progress and then stop. They cannot seem to get beyond a certain point. They can do only so much and no more. We see people in all walks of life never going beyond a certain point. There must be a reason for this.

When we look into the mental reason behind things,

we find out why they happen. Those who get only so far and never seem to go beyond that point are still governed by law. When they allow their thoughts to move out into larger fields of action, their conditions come up to their thought. When they stop enlarging their thought, they stop growing. If they would continue in thought, realizing more and still more, they would find that, in the outer form of things, they would be doing greater things.

There are many reasons why we stop thinking larger thoughts. One of them is lack of imagination. We cannot conceive of anything more to follow than that which has already happened. Another thought says, "This is as far as anyone can go in my business." Often people say, "I am too old to do bigger things." There they stop. Someone else might say, "The competition is too great," and here is where this person stops. We can go no further than our thought will carry us.

All this is unnecessary when we realize that life is first of all consciousness, then followed by conditions. There is no reason why we should not go on and never stop growing. No matter what age or what circumstance, if life is thought, we can keep thinking bigger things. There is no reason why we who are already doing well should not be able to conceive of a better condition. What if we are active? There is always a greater activity possible. We can still see a little beyond what has come before. This is just what we should do, even though it is a little beyond our former thought. If we always practice this, we will find that every year we will be growing, every month we will be advancing, and as time goes on, we will become really great. As there is no stopping in that power which is infinite, as the limitless is without bounds, so should we keep on trying to see more and greater possibilities in life.

We should work definitely every day for the expansion of thought. If we have fifty customers a day, we should endeavor to believe that we have sixty. When we have sixty, we should mentally see seventy. This should never stop, because there is no stopping place in mind.

Let go of and drop everything else from your thought. Mentally see more coming to you than has ever come before. Believe that mind is establishing this to you, and then go about your business in the regular way. Never see the limitation, never dwell on it, and above all else, never talk limitation to any one. This is the only way, and there is no other way, to grow a larger thought. The one with the big thought is always the one who does big things in life. Get a hold of the biggest thing that you can think of and claim it for your own. Mentally see it and hold it as a thing already done, and you will prove to yourself that life is without bounds.

ALWAYS BE GATHERING

❖ ❖ ❖

There is no reason why a person should ever stop. This does not mean that we should be miserly, trying to accumulate more and more, but that our thought should so enlarge that it cannot help gathering more and more, even though on the other hand—or *with* the other hand—we are distributing that which we gather. Indeed, the only reason for having is that we may give out of that which we have.

No matter what big thing happens to us, we should still be expecting more and more. Even when we think that we have at last arrived, right at the moment when it seems as though life has given us all that we could stand, right here, let it be only a beginning for still greater things.

No matter how large the picture is that you hold in mind, make it larger. The reason so many people stop is that they come to a point where they cease growing in their own minds. They come to a point where they can see no more, thinking that because they have done a big thing, they should stop there. We must watch our thought for signs of inactivity. Nothing in the universe ever stops. Everything is built on a boundless basis, drawn from a limitless source, coming forth from an infinite sea of unmanifest life. We speak into this life and draw back from it all that we first think into it. Life is always limitless, and the only thing that limits us is our inability to mentally conceive. We should draw more and more from that limitless source.

MENTAL LIKENESS

❖   ❖   ❖

We can draw from the infinite only as much as we first think into it. It is at this point that so many fail, thinking that all they need to do is to affirm what they want and it will follow. While it is true that affirmations have real power, it is also true that they have only that which we speak into them.

As we cannot speak a word that we do not know, so we cannot make an affirmation that we do not understand. We really affirm only that which we know to be true. We know to be true that which we have experienced within ourselves. Although we may have heard or read that this or that thing is true, it is only where there is something within our own souls that corresponds or recognizes its truth that it is true to us. This ought never to be lost sight of. We can effectively affirm only that which we know, and we know only that which we are. It is here that we see the necessity of providing within a greater concept of life, a bigger idea of ourselves, and a more expanded concept of the universe in which we live, move, and have our being. This is a matter of inner growth together with the enlarging of all lines of thought and activity.

If we want to do a thing that is really worth doing, we must mentally grow until we are the thing that we want to see made flesh. This may take time, but we should be glad to use all the time necessary to our own development.

Few people in limitation have a mental likeness of plenty. This likeness must be provided. The thought must be large enough to cover the whole of the thing desired. A small thought will produce only a small thing. The very fact that all is mind proves this to be true. All is mind, and, because it is, we can draw from that mind only that which we first think into it as a reality. We must become the thing that we want. We must see it, think it, and realize it before the creative power of mind can work it out for us. This is an inner process of the expansion of consciousness. It is a thought, growing and realizing within. Anyone can do this who wishes to and who will take the time and trouble, but it will mean work. Most people are too lazy to make the effort.

Daily, we must train our thought to see only what we wish to experience, and since we are growing into what we are mentally dwelling on, we should put all small and insignificant thoughts and ideas out of our thinking and see things in a larger way. We must cultivate the habit of an enlarged mental horizon, daily seeing further and further ahead and thus experiencing larger and greater things in our daily life.

A good practice for the enlargement of thought is to daily see yourself in a bigger place, filled with more activity and surrounded with increased influence and power. Feel more and more that things are coming to you. See that much more is just ahead and, as far as possible, know that you now have all that you see and feel. Affirm that you are that larger thing, that you are now entering into that larger life. Feel that something within is drawing more to you. Live with the idea and let the concept grow, expecting only the biggest and the best to happen. As you never let small thoughts come into your mind, you will soon find that a larger and greater experience has come into your life.

Keeping the Thing in Mind

❖   ❖   ❖

Never let go of the mental image until it becomes manifested. Daily, bring up the clear picture of what is wanted and impress it on the mind as an accomplished fact. As we impress on our minds the thought of what we wish to realize, it will cause our own minds to impress the same thought on universal mind. In this way, we will be praying without ceasing. We do not have to continually hold the thought of something we want in order to get it, only the thought that we may inwardly become the thing we want. Fifteen minutes twice a day is time enough to spend in order to demonstrate anything, but the rest of our time ought also to be spent constructively. That is, we must stop all negative thinking and give over all wrong thought, holding fast to the realization that it is now done unto us.

We must know that we are dealing with the only power there is in the universe, that there is none other beside it, and that we are partaking of its nature and its laws. Always, the calm confidence in our ability to speak into the power must be behind the word that we send forth, as well as the willingness of mind to execute for us. We must gradually grow in confidence and trust in the unseen world of spiritual activity. This is not difficult if we remember that the Spirit makes things out of itself by simply becoming the thing that it makes, and since there is no other power to oppose it, it will always work. The Spirit will never fail us if we never fail to believe in its goodness and its responsiveness.

Life will become one grand song when we realize that since God is for us, none can be against us. We will cease to merely exist; we will live.

Destroy Unwanted Thought

✦ ✦ ✦

We must resolutely set our faces to the rising consciousness of the truth. Seeing only the one power, we must destroy the adversary and leave the field to God, or good. All that is in any way negative must be wiped off the slate, and we must daily come into the higher thought to be washed clean of the dust and chaos of the objective life. In the silence of the soul's communion with the great source of all being, into the stillness of the Absolute, into the secret place of the Most High, behind the din and ceaseless roar of life, we will find a resting place and a place of real spiritual power. Speak in this inner silence and say, "I am one with Almighty. I am one with all life, with all power, and with all presence. I am. I am. I am."

Listen to the silence. From out of the seeming void, the voice of peace will answer the waiting soul, "All is well."

Here we make known all our needs and wants, and here we receive firsthand from the infinite all that we will ever need to make life healthy, happy, and harmonious. Few enter here because of the belief that conditions and circumstances control. Know that there is no law but God's law. The soul sets its own law in the infinite, and our slightest wish is honored of the mind.

Daily practice the truth, and daily die to all erroneous thought. Spend more time receiving and realizing the presence of the Most High and less time worrying. Wonderful power will come to those who believe and trust the power in which they have come to believe. Know that all good and all God is with you, all life and all power, and never again say, "I fear," but always, "I trust," because "I know in whom I have believed."

DIRECT PRACTICE FOR PROSPERITY

❖   ❖   ❖

Suppose that you are doing a mail order business and sending out promotional pieces across country. Take the pieces in your hands, or simply think of them, and declare into the mind that they will accomplish that for which they are sent out. Know that every word written on them is truth and carries its own conviction with it. See them each reaching that place where they will be received with gladness and read with interest. Declare this to be so now. Feel it to be the truth.

Mentally assert that each piece will find its way to the exact place where it will be wanted and where it will benefit the receiver. Feel that each piece is cared for by the Spirit, that it is a messenger of truth and power, and that it will carry conviction and realization with it.

When the word is spoken, feel that mind at once takes it up and never fails to act on it. Our place in the creative order is to know this and be willing to do all that we can without hurry or worry, and above all else, to trust absolutely in the Spirit to do the rest. The one who sees most clearly and believes most implicitly will make the greatest demonstration. This one should be you, and it will be you as soon as the false thought is gone and the realization comes that there is one power and one presence. We are wrapped in infinite love and intelligence, and we should cover ourselves with it and claim its protection from all evil. Declare that your word is the presence and the activity of the power of all that is, and wait for the perfect concept to unfold.

Race Consciousness

❖   ❖   ❖

One of the things that greatly hinders us from demonstrating a greater degree of prosperity is called *race thought*, or *race consciousness*. This is the result of all that the human race has thought or believed. We are immersed in it, and those who are receptive to it are controlled by it.

All thought seeks expression along the lines of least resistance. When we become negative or fearful, we attract that type of thought and condition. We must be sure ourselves. We must be positive, not aggressive, but absolutely sure and poised within.

Negative people are always picking up negative conditions. They get into trouble easily. People who are positive draw positive things. They are always successful. Few people realize that the law of thought is the great reality, that thoughts produce things. When we come to understand this power of thought, we will carefully watch our thinking to see that no thought enters that we should not want made into a thing.

We can guard our minds by knowing that no negative thought can enter. We can daily practice by saying that no race thought of limitation can enter the mind, that Spirit forms itself around us and protects us from all fear and from all limitation. Let us clothe ourselves in the great realization that all power is ours and that nothing else can enter. Let us fill the atmosphere of our homes and places of business with streams of positive thought. Other people will feel this and will want to be near us and enter into the things that we enter into. In this way, we will be continually drawing the best.

DEVELOPING INTUITION

❖ ❖ ❖

If we always lived close to mind, we would never make any great mistakes. Some seem to have the faculty of always knowing just what is best to do. They always succeed because they avoid making errors. We can all train ourselves so that we will be guided by the supreme mind of the universe, but we cannot do this until we believe that we can receive directly from the source of all knowledge. This is done by sitting in the silence and knowing that Spirit is inwardly directing us. We should try to feel that our thought is being permeated by the thought of the Spirit. We should expect it to direct, but should never become discouraged if a direct impression is not received immediately. The work is going on even if it is not seen or even felt. Thought is forming in our mind and, in time, will come forth as an idea. When the idea does come, always trust in it, even though it may not seem to be quite as we had expected. The first impressions are usually the most direct and the clearest. They are generally directly from the mind of the universe and should be carefully worked out into expression.

As we sit in the silence, we declare that the Spirit of knowledge is making known within us just what we should do, that it is telling us just what to say or where to go. Have absolute reliance on this, because it is one of the most important things to do. We should always get that inner assurance before undertaking any new enterprise, being sure that we have really put the whole thing into the hands of life and that all we have to do is to work it out in the outer. We will learn to avoid mistakes when we learn to be directed by that inner voice that never makes mistakes. We should declare in the silence that intelligence is guiding us, and it will do so.

Presence of Activity

❖ ❖ ❖

What if your place of business does not seem to manifest any activity? What if customers do not come? To those in the business world, the presence of customers generally means activity. Suppose that you have come to believe that the principle will work in the smallest as well as the greatest things. What you want now is a greater activity. How are you going to see activity when there is none yet? Must we overlook that which we see and that which we have experienced? Yes, absolutely! There is no other way.

If we keep on seeing the thing as it appears, we will never be able to change its appearance. What we must do, then, in spite of the seeming inactivity, is to still know and mentally see and declare that we are in the midst of activity. Feel this to be true. Mentally see your business as busy. Know that it is packed full of customers all the time. Declare that your word draws in customers. Have no sense of strain about it whatsoever. Simply know that you are dealing with the only power that there is. It will work. It must work.

Realize that when you have spoken the word, a greater power has taken it up and it is being established to you. Have no idea of limitation. Speak forth into mind with perfect trust. If you have the ability to mentally see your business full, combine this with the word and daily visualize it as being filled. Always combine faith in the higher power with all that you do. Feel that you are being especially looked after. This is true.

When a soul turns to the universe of unmanifest life, it turns at the same time toward the soul. Jesus told this in the story of the prodigal, when the father saw the son coming from far off. Always, there is that inward turning toward us of the parent mind when we turn to it and place ourselves in closer contact with life.

We must keep our mind clear so that when the Spirit brings the gift, we will be open to receive it. Even God cannot force things upon us. We must receive even before we see.

When we believe, we will always have that belief

honored by the Spirit of life, mentally seeing just what we want, still seeing even though the heavens fall. We will succeed in proving that the law of life is the law of liberty. God made us to have all that the universe contained and then left us alone to discover our own nature.

Stop all striving and struggle, and within your own soul know the truth and trust absolutely in it. Daily, declare that you are being guided and protected and that the power of the Spirit is bringing it to pass, and wait in perfect peace and confidence. Such an attitude of mind will overcome anything and will prove that spiritual thought force is the only real power in the universe.

DRAWING YOUR OWN TO YOU

❖　❖　❖

Suppose that you wish to draw friends and companions to you, that you wish to enlarge your circle of friendships. This, too, can all be worked out by law, because everything can be worked out by the same law, the reason being that all is one and that the one becomes the many in expression.

There are too many people in the world who are lonesome because they have a sense of separation from people. The thing to do is not to try to unify with people, but to unify with the principle of life behind all people and things. This is working from the center and not from the circumference. In this one mind are the minds of all people. When you unite your thought with the whole, you will be united with the parts of the whole.

The first thing to do, then, is to realize that life is your friend and companion. Feel the divine companionship. Feel that you are one with all life. Declare that as this thought awakens within your mind, so does it awaken within the mind of the whole human race. Feel that the world is being drawn to you. Love the world and everyone who is in it. Include all if you want to be included in all. The world seeks strength. Be strong. The world loves love. Embody it. See the good in all people. Let go of all else. People will feel your love and will be drawn to it. Love is the greatest power in the universe. It is at the base of all else. It is the cause. Feel your love to be like a great light illuminating the pathway of the whole world. It will come back to you, bringing so many friends that there will not be enough time to enjoy them all. Become a real friend, and you will have many friends.

Be sufficient unto yourself and, at the same time, include everyone else, and people will feel your strength and will have a desire to come into the radiance of it. Never become unhappy or morbid. Always be cheerful and radiate good nature and happiness. Never look depressed or down in the mouth. The world is attracted to the strongest center of cheer and good community. Never allow your feelings to be hurt. No one wants to hurt you, and no one could, even though they may seem to want to. You are above all that. Wherever you go, know that the Spirit of truth goes before and prepares the way, bringing to you every friend and influence that will be necessary for your comfort and well being. This is not selfishness, but good sense, and will surely bring to you a harvest of friends and companions.

Declare into mind that you are now linked with all people and all people are linked with you. See yourself surrounded with hosts of friends. Mentally feel their presence and rejoice that all good is yours now. Do this no matter what seems to happen, and it will not be long before you meet wonderful friends and will brought into touch with the great of the world.

THE FINAL WORD

✦   ✦   ✦

In the last analysis, we are only what we think ourselves to be. We are big in capacity if we think big thoughts; we are small if we think small thoughts. We will attract to ourselves what we think most about. We can govern our own destiny when we learn to control our thoughts. In order to do this, we must first realize that everything in the manifest universe is the result of some inner activity of mind. This mind is God, producing a universe by the activity of God's own divine thoughts. We are in this mind as thinking centers, and what we think governs our lives, even as God's thoughts govern the universe by setting in motion all the cosmic activities. This is so easy to understand and so simple to use that we often wonder why we have been so long in finding out this greatest of all truths of all the ages. These are the steps that, when followed, will bring us to where we will not have to ask if they are true, because having demonstrated, we will know. Believe. Think what is believed to be true. Think into mind each day that which is wished to be returned. Eliminate negative thoughts. Hold all positive thoughts. Give thanks to the Spirit of life that it is trusting always in the higher law. Never argue with one's self or with others. Use it.

The seed that falls into the ground will bear fruit of its own kind, and nothing will hinder it.

"Those who have ears to hear, let them hear."

The End

About the Author

Ernest Shurtleff Holmes (1887–1960), an ordained Divine Science minister, was founder of a spiritual movement known as Religious Science, a part of the New Thought movement, whose spiritual philosophy is known as Science of Mind. He was the author of *The Science of Mind* and numerous other metaphysical books, as well as founder of *Science of Mind* magazine, in continuous publication since 1927.

Original editions of classic books, such as *Creative Mind and Success,* written by Ernest Holmes in 1922, hold great value as documents that not only give us the information we want, but do so in a way that imparts a sense of the time in which they were written, through language usage, idiom, even punctuation. Yet there is value in revising and updating book manuscripts from the past. With skilled editing, new editions of classic books can invigorate the manuscript and clear up language that can be challenging to understand today, while at the same time, retain the author's distinctive voice and intention. Such is the case with the books of Newt List.

Newt List offers updated editions of spiritual classic texts. Newt List titles have been edited to provide contemporary language structure and idioms that have evolved since the original manuscript was published. We revise punctuation and capitalizations, and adjust sentence structure when appropriate, as well as update certain words or terms that have since become obscure, as long as those changes do not affect the author's intention or expression.

More valuable for readers today, though, is Newt List's procedure of updating gender forms. In the time of original publication, these classic books generally used masculine forms when referring to God or humankind. Newt List edits all its books using gender-neutral language, making the ideas in them apply more broadly to all readers.

If you have never read these amazing books in their original editions, you are in for a great adventure—a new way of thinking about life. If you *have* read these books before, Newt List thinks you will find that our books come alive in original and fresh ways which make the ideas in them more immediate, relevant, and, more importantly, life changing.

For more books by Ernest Holmes
and other New Thought authors,
visit NewtList.com.

If you enjoyed Ernest Holmes' Creative Mind and Success,
you may enjoy these other fine Newt List titles.

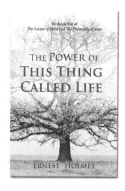

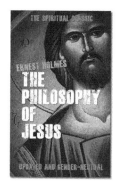

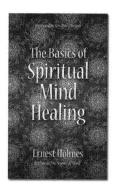

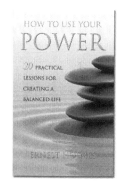

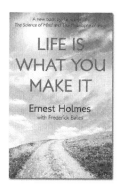

www.NewtList.com